# How BIKES Work

## by Judy Healy

PEARSON
Scott
Foresman

# What You Already Know

Science studies movement. An object changes position when it moves. Scientists compare objects in motion to other objects. The relative position of an object is where it is compared to other objects.

Speed is how fast an object changes position. Speed depends on force. Force is a push or pull that moves an object. Most forces are contact forces. Friction is a contact force that works against the motion of an object. Friction also affects the speed of a moving object.

Speed also depends on the weight of the object. An empty wagon rolls easily down a road. The more objects that fill the wagon, the heavier it becomes. This makes it harder to pull and slows its speed.

Gravity is a non-contact force. All objects on Earth are pulled toward Earth's center by the force of gravity. Magnetism is another non-contact force. It is a strong force that pulls at certain kinds of metals, such as those containing iron.

In science, the word *work* has a special meaning. Work is done when force moves an object. People have invented simple machines to do the same amount of work with less force.

Riding a bicycle is work. In this book you will learn about the bicycle and what happens to make the work of riding possible. The bicycle uses force from the rider to change the rider's position. Let's learn how!

# Marvelous Machines

Bicycles are marvelous machines. They help us move faster and more easily than we can on foot. Look at the bicycles in the picture. What do you see? Can you name all the different parts of a bicycle? Do you see handlebars? What about wheels? Where are the pedals, gears, and axles? In the next few pages you will learn about these parts and how they make it possible for you to ride a bike.

Scientists who study how objects move are called physicists. These scientists study the force, friction, work, and motion of objects large and small. Physicists help us understand how bicycles work.

Engineers are scientists who design and build machines. Bicycle engineers study physics to try to improve bicycle designs. Now we will study the physics and uses of bicycles!

Bikes are a lot of fun to ride.
They are useful machines.

# Motion Magnifier

Like a Ferris wheel or merry-go-round, a bicycle uses a wheel and axle. Our leg muscles push on pedals that are attached to a chain. The chain is attached to the back wheel of the bike. The chain spins the back axle. The axle is a bar that connects the wheel to the bike.

**There are many different parts of a bicycle. Do you know them all?**

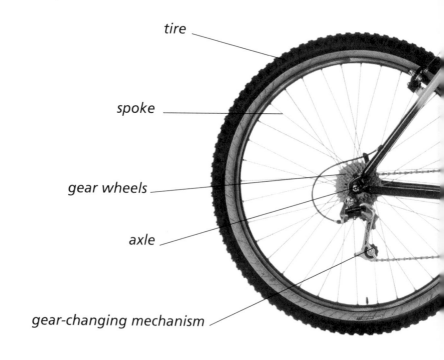

tire

spoke

gear wheels

axle

gear-changing mechanism

The axle spins in a small circle. It moves the back wheel in a large circle. The small spinning of the axle is magnified in the large spinning of the wheel. So the back axle and wheel receive all the force of our leg muscles. The front wheel is used for balance and steering. The back wheel does all the work.

seat

handlebar

brake lever

water bottle

brake cable

brake block

pedal

chain wheel

chain

# Geared Up

Gears are an important part of a bicycle. Different gears work best using different amounts of force. Gears allow you to pedal the right amount for the terrain you are riding on.

The gears are the smaller wheels near the axle. They are called the gear wheels. This is where the chain is attached. The chain also fits on two or three larger different-sized wheels near the pedals. These are called the chain wheels.

**When cyclists bike uphill, they often switch to a lower gear.**

## How Gears Work

This drawing shows two different chain wheels from the same bike. In lowest gear, the smallest chain wheel is connected to the largest gear wheel. In highest gear, the largest chain wheel is connected to the smallest gear wheel.

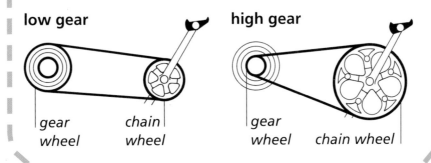

low gear

gear wheel    chain wheel

high gear

gear wheel    chain wheel

A bicycle with many gears has different-sized chain wheels and gear wheels. In high gear, you need more force to turn the large chain wheel. But this spins the back wheel faster. In low gear, you need less force to turn the small chain wheel. But this spins the back wheel more slowly.

It is much easier to spin the smaller chain wheel. Lots of cyclists switch to low gear when going uphill. The largest gear wheel moves slowly, moving the rear wheel and the bicycle slowly. This makes uphill cycling slower but easier.

# Keeping Balance

Can you ride a bike without training wheels? How did you learn? Did you fall a lot when you learned? It takes practice to learn to ride a bike without training wheels.

To ride a bike, you have to learn how to balance. To balance on a bike, most of your body must be above the point where the tires meet the ground. If you lean too far one way, gravity will pull you to the ground on that side. Bicycle engineers must make sure the seat is put in the right place. Otherwise, it would be hard to balance.

**Balancing on a bike takes practice.**

Some people race their bicycles around oval tracks. Riding around the curves in the track involves a force that pushes the bicycles toward the center of the oval. Leaning toward the center balances this force and the one that is tending to keep the riders moving in a straight line. The curves in the track are often raised on the outside so that the surface is at a slant. The slanted surface pushes the riders toward the center while keeping the wheels from slipping.

Some cyclists race on long courses, often over hills or even mountains. These riders must learn to ride across the slopes of hills. Picture a hill near your home. Now think about riding across the hill. Which way will gravity be pulling you? Downhill. To ride across slopes, cyclists lean into the hill. This keeps their center of gravity on top of the wheels so that the bike will stay upright against the pull of gravity.

# Get a Grip!

There are many different forces working against each other when a bike is moving. Terrain, wheel traction, and wind all create friction. Smooth tires grip smooth roads well. Rough tires grip rough roads well. But smooth tires slip on rough terrain since they do not have enough friction. Rough tires create too much friction on smooth terrain, so cycling is slow and difficult.

**Rough tires help grip this rough terrain.**

When riding downhill, cyclists can pick up so much speed that they need to use brakes to slow down. Brakes create friction that slows down a moving bike. Most brake controls are on the handlebars. Some bicycles have back-pedal brakes.

**road tire**

**off-road tire**

## How Brakes Work

Hand brakes rest on both sides of the wheel. When you pull the controls, the brakes pinch the wheel. This makes friction that slows down the bike wheel.

**caliper brakes**

# Reducing Friction

Racing cyclists try to cut down on friction so they are able to ride faster. Racing cyclists lean very low on their bikes. This lowers the amount of friction from wind that hits the cyclists' bodies. Even racing cyclists' clothes and helmets are made to reduce friction from wind.

**Racing cyclists lean forward to reduce friction from wind.**

Some types of friction can be dangerous. When chain wheels, gear wheels, and axles spin, they rub against metal parts. Where these metal pieces rub one another, friction results. This friction causes the metals to wear away. This kind of damage is dangerous when it causes the parts to break or stop working.

**Putting oil on metal reduces friction and makes spinning easier.**

## How Bearings Work

Bearings are smooth, metal balls that roll easily. They are used in places to reduce friction where two metals rub against each other. Instead of the two metals rubbing, the bearings roll against the metal. There is less friction with rolling bearings.

**bearings inside a bike**

# Riding the Bumps

Bicycle wheels were once made of wood or metal. Think about riding on a bumpy road with wooden or metal wheels! They would not flex or bend, so you would feel every pebble. Modern bicycles are designed to make riding smooth and comfortable. Tires are made of rubber and filled with air. This helps absorb some of the bumps. When the tire hits a pebble, the soft, air-filled tube absorbs the bump so you don't feel it on your body.

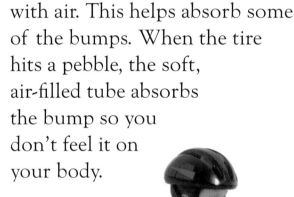

**These girls are filling this bicycle tire with air using a hand pump.**

Some bicycles also have suspensions. A suspension is a system of springs. Some bicycles have springs on the front wheel, others on the rear. Some bicycles have springs in the seats. Springs make riding more comfortable by absorbing bumps just like the tires. It is still important to watch out for large holes and rocks.

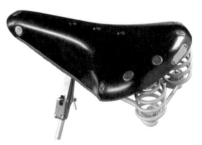

sprung seat

padded seat

# Designed for Safety

Bicycles are designed for speed and comfort, but most importantly for safety. Reflectors are put on bikes so the rider can be seen in the dark. Most reflectors are white, orange, or red. They are tiny lenses that reflect light from a car's headlights back to the car's driver. This helps the driver see the cyclist. Bicycles must have reflectors. They are often on the back, front, and pedals of bicycles.

**reflector**

Many bicycles also have front and backlights. Front lights shine down on the path in front of the rider. This way riders can see where they are riding at night. The light also warns cars that a cyclist is there. Backlights are often red, like the backlights on cars. They flash on and off, warning cars behind the rider.

**putting on a helmet**

You can see small reflectors on pedals because they move very quickly.

All cyclists should wear safety gear. Helmets are the most important because they protect cyclists from hurting their heads. Gloves help cyclists grip the handlebars to keep control of the bicycle. Reflective clothing helps others see cyclists.

Whether you are cycling in the daytime or at nighttime, it is always important to have safety gear.

Front lights are like small car headlights.

Backlights are often red and flashing.

# Types of Bikes

There are three main types of bicycles. They each have a special design and use. Road or racing bicycles are made for riding on smooth roads. What features of the racing bicycle shown below are made for smooth, fast travel? Notice that the wheels are thin and smooth. This cuts down on friction so the bicycle moves faster. The handlebars are curled so the cyclist can lean forward to reduce friction from the wind.

**Racing bicycles are made for speed.**

Mountain bicycles are made for rough riding. Many mountain bikers race on rough, muddy, and bumpy land. What features of the mountain bicycle shown below are made for rough riding? Notice the wheels are thick and have ridges. The thick wheels make the bike strong. The ridges of the wheels dig into loose or muddy soil. This creates the friction that keeps the cyclist up straight. The wide handlebars help the cyclist stay balanced.

**Mountain bicycles are made for rough riding.**

**BMX bikes are small and light.**

The other main type of bicycle is the dirt or BMX bike. (BMX stands for Bicycle Motocross—the type of racing these bikes are made for.) Like the mountain bike, the BMX bike is made for riding on rough ground. Most BMX bicycles are used for trick riding. BMX riders often race on dirt courses. BMX bicycles are small and light, so riders can lift the bikes over jumps. The BMX frame is also strong so it can handle tough motocross racing.

Two other interesting types of bicycles are tandem and folding bikes. Tandem bicycles are built for two people. Two cyclists pedal and both create force and speed. Tandem biking is also a fun way to spend time with someone.

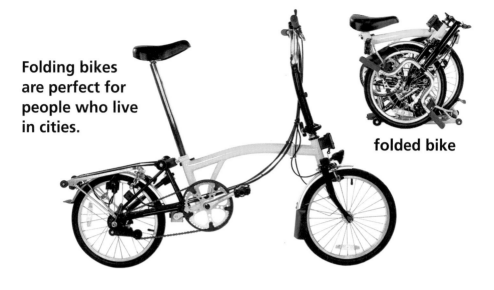

**Folding bikes are perfect for people who live in cities.**

**folded bike**

Folding bikes are helpful in cities. People who ride bikes to work in cities must fit them in small office spaces.

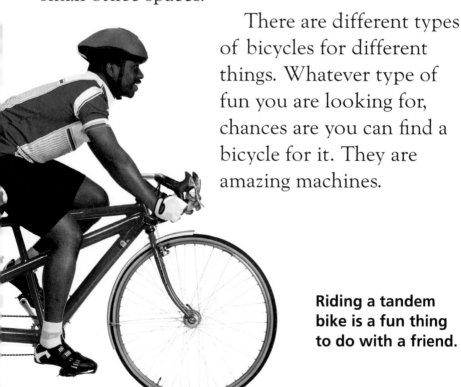

There are different types of bicycles for different things. Whatever type of fun you are looking for, chances are you can find a bicycle for it. They are amazing machines.

**Riding a tandem bike is a fun thing to do with a friend.**

# Glossary

**absorb**  to take in and make a part of

**center of gravity**  point in an object or person where weight is balanced

**contracts**  shortens or squeezes

**reflectors**  objects that throw back light, heat, or sound

**slope**  upward or downward slant of a hill

**terrain**  the physical features of a trail or surface

**traction**  surface friction that prevents slipping